A Maritime History of FOWEY HARBOUR

'A Fair and Commodious Haven'

Helen Doe

truran

*In memory of my mother and for
my sisters Susan and Fiona*

ISBN 978 185022 232 3

Published by Truran, Water Lane, St Agnes TR5 0RA

Truran is an imprint of Truran Books Ltd
www.truranbooks.co.uk

© Helen Doe 2010

Image © as indicated

Designed by Alix Wood www.alixwood.co.uk

Printed and bound in Cornwall by R Booth Ltd, The Praze, Penryn TR10 8AA

Fowey Harbour and its People across the Centuries

FOWEY HARBOUR AND THE settlements within it exist because of the sea and its importance rests on the sea. Stand by the water's edge at any place in the harbour and you can see in your mind's eye the ships that came and went throughout the centuries. Mariners and merchants travelled in and out of the estuary, goods arrived at the quays and passengers gratefully stepped on shore or left on their voyages. Boatmen and barges travelled up and down the river and across the harbour transporting goods and people to ocean going ships. The ferry service has long been a critical and essential element in the harbour carrying passengers between Polruan and Fowey and people, goods, livestock, horses and carriages between Bodinnick and Fowey. In any coastal community the sea is the essential communications route to other places. Before trains and air transport, goods and people moved with difficulty along narrow roads that were frequently muddy and pot-holed. Waterborne transport was the most effective method and all roads led to the sea where ships of all sizes provided vital links along the coast and across the oceans.

Geography plays an important role in the success of communities. Fowey harbour is one of the largest natural harbours on the south coast which made it a natural trading point, harbour of refuge in bad weather and a gathering place for fleets of ships. Over the centuries the nearness of France and Spain has been both a trading benefit and a severe threat in times of war. The River Fowey links the harbour with Lostwithiel six miles up stream. As Lostwithiel was an important medieval town Fowey was its main outlet to the wider world. The story of the harbour over the centuries is rich and varied and full of incident. The people of the harbour have played their part in great events and seen great success but they have also known hard times. Here are just some of the events in a long, rich and distinguished past.

Lostwithiel Bridge from where the jurisdiction of the 'Waters of Fowey' begins (HD) ▷

An Important Harbour

WITH A NATURAL DEEP water harbour and a situation close to France, Spain and Portugal, trade has always been important. Additionally, Cornwall's tin and copper were already in demand in the Mediterranean in the Bronze Age. It has been suggested that places such as Readymoney, just inside the harbour, and Pridmouth and Coombe, situated just outside, may have been early trading centres. Polruan Pool provided an early natural sheltered mooring site.[1]

The early medieval period has left a few more traces and a sixth century memorial, known as the Tristan stone, is an important relic that has been connected with the Tristan and Isolde legend. Such a memorial emphasises the importance of Fowey as strategic place of power in the period. Churches, too, were symbols of power in a different context and it has been traditionally considered that Christianity was brought to Cornwall by saints such as Cadoc, Piran and Sampson. While several aspects of the lives of the saints have been challenged, as the biographies of these saints were written in many cases over 200 years later, they do show the early connections between Brittany, Cornwall, Wales and Ireland.[2]

Fowey, Bodinnick and Polruan have always been closely connected. The Bodinnick and

△ Bodinnick Ferry and the Ferry Inn (Truran)

Medieval houses with own access to wharfs and the water (Truran) ▷

Fowey connection exists because of the southern route through Cornwall. Travellers crossed the Tamar by ferry and arrived at the Bodinnick crossing. The Bodinnick ferry crossing possibly dates from the fourteenth century and for the weary traveller arriving from the east the requirement for a place of refreshment while waiting for the ferryman naturally led to the need for a hostelry and so the Ferry Inn will certainly have had its early predecessor. Polruan may have had poorer inland communications but it was an important early settlement because it had the sheltered anchorage. The existence of the chapel of St Saviour's and the position of the parish church well inland are other indicators of this. The antecedents of the Polruan ferry are also likely to go back into the early medieval period.[3]

The connections with the sea brought early trading contacts and in the medieval period Fowey was the most important port town in Cornwall and one of the most important in England. There were several reasons for this in addition to its advantages to shipping as a natural deep water port. By the late thirteenth century Lostwithiel had become the centre of the administration of the earldom of Cornwall. Lostwithiel was also the main market for tin and Cornwall was the known world's largest supplier of that valuable commodity. There was greater awareness of the strategic significance of the Cornish coast in maritime matters. In 1268 Earl Richard gained authority over Lostwithiel, the waters of Fowey, the Tamar and also the ports of Saltash and Plymouth harbour.

So, until the nineteenth century the waters of Fowey were controlled by Lostwithiel. Tin was coined (assayed and stamped as tax paid) in Lostwithiel and shipped by barge to Fowey and then transhipped aboard larger ships for export. This outward trade helped Fowey to grow in importance. Lostwithiel, however, retained control of any dues paid by shipping using the harbour of Fowey and was also a base for a maritime court. Due to the international nature of shipping, disputes between shipowners, masters, mariners and merchants of all nationalities could arise in a number of ways through collision, fraud, mismanagement or war. This led to the earliest international system of law, maritime law. Disputes were handled by special maritime courts, locally in Lostwithiel or Fowey or for serious matters, in London.

When the Black Prince, son of Edward III, became the first Duke of Cornwall, he brought the Duchy and its revenues to the Crown where it remains. Fowey by now had borough status, held its own fair and market and was home to a growing number of merchants. They were attracted to ports as the trade with the continent grew. These merchants needed a location to store the goods while waiting for transport, men to load and unload the goods and a regular supply of ships with experienced masters. The merchants built houses and warehouses and small quays developed to facilitate the turn around of the ships. Various taxes were levied on goods, both imported and exported, and the man responsible for the administration of the income from Cornwall was the havener. The Black Prince appointed Thomas Fitz Henry as the first havener to the Duchy. He served the Prince for an impressive 35 years and was based in Fowey on the Town Quay.

Fitz Henry was a salaried official and amongst his duties was the right of wreck, which was to ensure the wreck was properly valued, supervise salvage, ensure a percentage went to the Duchy and that pillagers were fined. Another tax was prisage which was the lord's right to one or two tuns (large wine barrels) from each ship docking at the port and was usually commuted to a fee. Fishing was yet another revenue source for the Duchy and Fowey is shown as a fishing port by the payment of £2 tax paid to the Duchy and Polruan paid £1. Fishing was not as significant in Fowey when compared with the ports of Mousehole and St Ives, which paid £5 and £6 respectively. The havener was also involved in maritime law disputes and these could include such incidents as the Plymouth merchant who sold a ship in Bruges for 500 marks and omitted to pay the ship-owner, there were fines for using the wrong kind of nets or for fishing out of season and disputes with Spanish fishermen.[4]

Today, one curious remnant from earlier times is Punches Cross, which is a white painted wooden cross on the rocks on the Polruan side of the entrance to the harbour. No clear evidence has yet been found to explain its existence or when the first cross was sited there. One of the theories is that this was the limit of the jurisdiction of the priory of Tywardreath. Tywardreath Priory was established in the twelfth century and was an off shoot of an abbey at Angers. Staffed initially with seven monks, it was part of the establishment of French religious houses in Cornwall to which it owed both allegiance and funding. The Hundred Years War with France challenged their allegiance to that country and they were designated as 'alien' priories and their activities were restricted. Movable assets and revenue were diverted to the English Crown rather than to France and eventually in 1378 all foreign monks were ordered to leave. This caused the priories such as Tywardreath to struggle for survival.[5]

△ Polruan from the water (Truran)

If the cross dates from this early period it is unlikely to have been connected with the priory which had little power. It is more likely that the cross was placed to denote the bounds of the medieval port of St Saviour's, first mentioned in the will of Edmund Earl of Cornwall in 1269 and named after the chapel on the Polruan headland and below which the cross is sited. Polruan was first mentioned in the thirteenth century and it had the sheltered anchorage. The chapel of St Saviour's, situated high on the hill, dates from that time. The chapel with its high tower was an effective day mark for ships approaching the harbour.

The start of the 100 Years War and the granting of Fowey, Plymouth and Dartmouth to the Black Prince increased the importance of these strategically placed ports. Fowey, in particular was often used by the Black Prince (whose headquarters were at Lostwithiel) to provide local shipmasters, pilots, mariners to move men and arms to France. This gave a boost to shipbuilding and other trades in the port. At this time, Polruan was a significant place in its own right and, together with Fowey, was a regular provider of ships for royal service. Ships were supplied from Fowey as in the 1326 attack on Norman shipping when two vessels from Fowey are included in a list of ships summoned for service by Edward III. In 1340 ships present at the battle of Sluys, considered to be the first naval battle, included six Fowey ships and one from Polruan. By 1343 nine Fowey ships and five Polruan ships were mentioned for the King's service and four years later a very large fleet of 47 ships assembled to support the siege of Calais. This was a high point for Fowey as they provided more ships than any other port. The ability to provide and man so many large ships for war demonstrates the influence of the port and the regular mention of Polruan ships indicates its wealth at the time. Other major suppliers of both men and ships for sea service in England were Great Yarmouth and the Cinque ports and there were great rivalries between the ports. The Cinque Ports and Great Yarmouth were bitter enemies and admirals were given special orders to keep the fleets apart and this puts the oft quoted raid by Fowey on the Cinque Ports in 1330 into a slightly different context.[6] It seems such happenings were part of the jealousies between ports.

Table 1: Ships supplied for Royal Service

	1326	1340	1343	1347
Fowey	2	6	9	47
Polruan		1	5	1
Dartmouth	10	9	10	31
Plymouth	3	6	9	26
London	3	10	15	25

N.A.M. Rodger, *The Safeguard of the Sea* (London: Penguin, 2004). p. 497.

Medieval Trade

THE SHIPS OF FOWEY harbour were busy in both coastal and foreign trades. While the coastal trade was important, taking tin and other cargoes to London or Southampton, other trades grew in significance. From the late fifteenth century Fowey had trade with Ireland taking salt out and returning with fish such as hake and flat fish. Despite strong competition from other ports, Fowey was the biggest trading port in Cornwall and imported more grain and salt than any other and exported hides, tin and fish. Ships were highly flexible methods of transport carrying varied commodities. The masters required thorough knowledge of how to stow the casks, bales, bundles, packs, baskets and, on occasions, horses and, of course, people. Wine importation was another significant trade. From 1307 to 1449 Fowey ships dominated the Cornish wine trade with 56 per cent of all ships. The English under the Plantagenets controlled large parts of France including Bordeaux and much of Aquitaine came under English control with the marriage of Eleanor to Henry II. Of the 74 wine ships trading from Fowey harbour between 1332 and 1356, thirty five were owned in Fowey, nineteen from Polruan, fourteen from Bodinnick and even Lostwithiel (to which such ships could not reach) owned six.[7] Ten major shipments per year in the wine trade were normal.

Large ships were required for the wine trade and in 1308 one Fowey ship loaded 107 tuns (one tun held about 250 gallons). They not only brought wine in to Fowey, but they also worked as carriers for other ports taking wine to Chester for instance.[8] Such large and heavily built ships were very valuable to the Crown. In 1451 a naval impressment rated the *Barry* of Fowey at 300 tuns, Walter Wymonde's *Cog John* at 240 tuns and Robert Lante's *Julian* at 200 tons. Robert Lante is a good example of how one man could progress in his career. In 1428 he was the master of the *Trinity* of Fowey owned by John Spert taking pilgrims to Corunna. Between 1431 and 1445 he is recorded as making four voyages to Bordeaux and by 1449 was himself the owner of the *Julian* of Fowey. This ship carried a crew of 32 and by this stage he was able to employ a master.[9] If, however, he had made his money in the Bordeaux wine trade this was about to change. He and many others in Fowey were affected by a significant drop in trade in 1450 when Gascony was lost to the French and wine no longer came down river to Bordeaux.

There was another regular and profitable trade across the Bay of Biscay carrying pilgrims to the north coast of Spain to visit the shrine at Santiago de Compostela. It was a licensed trade so there are good records. Devon, Cornwall, Dorset and Somerset had 60 per cent of all the licensed shipping with Devon and Cornwall predominant. Most licences were issued between 1390 and 1460 when the King was endeavouring to police the licensing system. Special pilgrim voyages were arranged by shipowners, almost like some form of holiday excursion. Between 1427 and 1428 over 53 Westcountry ships carried 3,755 passengers. A surviving account for a London ship suggests that it could be a very lucrative business as the fee per passenger was 7s 6d return. The ships made fast passages, taking between three to four weeks and carried passengers each way. This was fast earning compared to trading voyages of several months and no certainty of goods on each leg. The larger ships of Fowey might expect to earn well. [10]

As a significant port, Fowey saw many important arrivals and departures during this time and an idea of the impact these had comes from the following example. John of Gaunt the younger brother of the Black Prince was based in Aquitaine as regent acting on behalf of the Prince. On 21st September 1371 John married Constance of Castile the exiled heiress to the throne of Portugal. They were married near Bordeaux and then proceeded to the port of La Rochelle to return to England. Here they requisitioned a salt ship, requiring the master to remove his cargo from the ship to provide space for their belongings and their retinue. As befitted their rank, John was one of the wealthiest and most powerful men in England, he was attended by a train of Castilian knights wearing Lancastrian livery and Constance by a bevy of Castilian ladies. Their arrival in Fowey on 4th November must have been an impressive sight. From Fowey they moved to Plympton Priory from 10th to 14th November before travelling onwards to Exeter.[11]

The death of the Black Prince in 1376 was significant for the area as it was no longer such an important site for royal power. His son Richard II succeeded his grandfather, Edward III, as a minor and the subsequent tensions led to the seizure of his throne in 1399 by Henry IV, son of John Duke of Gaunt. Meanwhile trade, despite the decline of the wine trade from 1450, carried on as is evident from the customs reports for London in 1480 and 1481. Fowey ships arriving there carried a range of goods. Robert Laverok's ship *Edward* of Fowey imported 26 tuns of oil, 24 cases of sugar, one bale of grain from Portugal weighing 100 lbs and the total value was £144. Nicholas Barbour's ship *Kateryn* of Fowey brought in seven hogsheads of dates worth £17 10s; 30 bales of dates each weighing 1½ hundredweight worth £20, one bale Spanish grain weighing 336 lbs, worth £16 16s 8d and one bale of Seville grain weighing 150 lbs. worth £8 8s.4d.[12] The goods were destined for Portuguese and Italian merchants based in London. In the same period other Fowey ships were known to trade to the Baltic.

'The Sons of Iniquity'

UNTIL THE MIDDLE OF the fifteenth century few English kings needed to be overly concerned about security in the Channel as they had control of many of the continental ports. Piracy was the biggest risk to shipping and Henry V, a king who understood the importance of sea power, suppressed piracy ruthlessly. On his death in 1422 the practice revived rapidly and adopted the new type of carvel built ships. This century saw the Wars of the Roses, wars with France and the loss of Bordeaux in 1453. All these events had an impact on Fowey as the Crown took its eyes off Cornwall being too busy fighting its own battles both at home and abroad. Disruption of trade and loss of local royal influence led to increasing numbers of men turning to other ways of earning income and privateering and piracy thrived. Trained masters and mariners with their big armed ships took full advantage of the power vacuum to attack other vessels, usually ones they could loosely identify as enemies of the Crown although at times such justification was weak. It was, however, not always a clear cut distinction. The Crown encouraged privateering as strong well armed merchant ships were a useful defence during the 100 Years War when coastal raids were regular.

There were attacks on Fowey by Spanish fleets in 1378 and by Bretons and Normans in 1457. Over 80 years later Leland referred to the story of the French raid in 1457 and described how Elizabeth Treffry defended Place, the Treffry manor house, in the absence of her husband. Place was subsequently fortified and the two blockhouses were erected to protect the port. A chain was placed between the blockhouses which could be raised to prevent enemy ships entering the harbour. The blockhouses could also be armed. However the owners of ships in Fowey and Polruan were not just innocent victims of raids by other countries. They were well known to the courts for the number of cases brought against them by ship owners. Previous Fowey historians have told the tale of the loss of the chain in 1478

Place - the home of the Treffreys (Truran) ▷

due to the outrageous conduct of the Fowey pirates when the complaints caused the King to imprison the local burgesses (local officials) and the chain was removed and given to Dartmouth.[13]

The so-called pirates were very successful, but they were also well protected at a senior level. There were times when the Crown was only too happy to use such people and their ships for its own purposes. Mark Mixstowe (or Michaelstowe) of Fowey was known and feared throughout ports of Europe and yet his ship the *Mackerel* of Fowey belonged to Henry VI's Admiral of England, the Duke of Exeter.[14] Most of the notorious pirates were privateers, licensed by the King in times of war to attack the ships of the enemy. Mark Mixstowe seized sixteen French and Spanish ships in 1402 when he was in command of a squadron of Fowey ships 'sea keeping' against aggression from the French fleet.[15] John Russell of Fowey was also a privateer and he was involved in both the pilgrim trade and also for transporting troops and supplies for the King.[16] These men were opportunists who worked on both sides of the law when it suited them.

John Mixstowe, the son of Mark, carried on the family tradition and he is mentioned in 1433 accused of taking a ship sailing from Seville to Sandwich. The ship was captured off Cape St Vincent and the crew were put ashore in Portugal and the ship taken to Fowey. Mark's ship was the *Edward* of Polruan, carrying 200 men 'armed and arrayed for war' including Thomas Adam and John Waterman of Polruan, John Porth of St Austell, John

Perkyn, William Phelyppe, John and Martin Roch and John Evyll of Taunton. Unfortunately the ship was owned by a very disgruntled merchant from London, John Chirche who took the case to court by which time the goods had already been dispersed across Cornwall, Devon, Somerset and Wiltshire. The *Katherine* of Blavet from Brittany was loaded with salt and wine on its way to England in June 1440 during a time of truce between the two countries. It was seized by Thomas Norman, master of a balinger of Fowey. The *Seynt Cruce*, captured in 1452, was a Spanish vessel chartered by Peter Cryke of Bristol. It was carrying 80 tons of iron, wood and 'other merchandise of great value' and had a safe conduct for Bristol. Implicated in its capture were Thomas Adam of Polruan master of *Palmer*, Robert Hikkes, Thomas Philip, John Huysh merchant, John Hyshh seaman, master of *La Julyan of Fowey*, John Atterede, victualler and Walter Hill, a priest.[17]

The Treffry and Mixstowe families were connected by the marriage of Thomas Treffry to the Mixstowe heiress, Amicia or Avisia and they were implicated in the biggest case of alleged piracy. This was the seizure of the *St Anthony and St Francis* in 1450 and it was so notorious that the Bishop of Exeter was outraged and wrote: 'Many persons from our diocese, and particularly from Cornwall, evil men and sons of iniquity, did violently seize, remove and carry away a very large quantity of goods and merchandise from the galley.' The ship was owned in Spain but had been seized at Plymouth and goods to the value of £12,000 were spirited away from Fowey. Implicated in the capture were the *Edward* of Polruan and the *Mackerel* of Fowey and the names included Thomas Philip, John Attred, Thomas Gardiner, John Roger, Nicoll Skawyth, Walter Kilwhite, William Webb, John Trevelyn, plus Sir Hugh Courtney of Boconnoc, Thomas Treffry and John Mixtow. The Bishop's fury is understandable when the list of known receivers of the goods included, Thomas Treffry, John Trelawney of Pelynt, Thomas Edward, Vicar of St Pinnock, John Netherton, priest, Robert Ferrour, Vicar of Altarnun, John Achymn, Vicar of Pelynt and John Fenour, Vicar of Lanteglos by Fowey.[18] The boundaries between merchant, privateer and pirate were not always clear, but all of the cases demonstrate a very high level of skill in both seamanship and organisation.

There is one very interesting aspect to Fowey shipping in this period amidst all the apparent disorder of piracy. Ship technology was changing between 1400 and 1550. One big change was the move from a single mast to a three masted ship which enabled more flexible sail plans. There is a carving in St Winnow church on the banks of the River Fowey that shows this early development. It is in Fowey that there is the very first mention in Britain of the other major technological change in ship type, the carvel. Developed from the Portuguese caravel, this skeleton construction was to spread around Northern Europe in the fifteenth century. Where vessels like the cog were sturdy and heavy and limited in size by their construction, the skeleton construction of frame with hull planking would enable more versatile ships. The carvel in question was owned by John Stevens of Fowey between 1443 and 1450.[19] Fowey shipwrights were certainly in the vanguard of the changing times.

'Hauntid with Shippes'

THE GLORIE OF FOWEY,' wrote Leland (the Tudor traveller and historian) 'rose by the warres in King Edwarde the First and the Thirde, and Henry the V's day, partely by feates of warre, partely by pyracie, and so waxing riche felle al to marchaundize: so that the towne was hauntid with shippes of diverse nations, and their shippes went to al nations.' [20]

The arrival of the Tudor dynasty brought change to Cornwall with a more settled and central administration. Henry VII needed to gain control over his new kingdom and in 1488 he sent Sir Richard Edgcumbe to Ireland to persuade the Irish Earls to swear their allegiance to the new king. Sir Richard set out in June with 500 men in four ships including the *Anne of Fowey*. Henry wished to control piracy and illegal privateering and part of Sir Richard's mission was to search for rovers, that is pirates/privateers, around the Isles of Scilly. In particular, he was on the look out for a 'Fleming Shipp of Warr' that was menacing shipping in the Severn. Eventually Sir Richard crossed the Irish Sea to accomplish his main mission. After remaining for some weeks his small fleet set sail again on 31st July but encountered severe storms. On their arrival in Polruan on August 8th, grateful for their safe deliverance, Sir Richard landed and went on pilgrimage to give thanks at the Chapel of St Saviour's. The storm must indeed have been severe as he subsequently paid for the enlargement of the chapel in gratitude.[21]

The Treffry family were strong supporters of the Tudors. Such closeness meant that they were in a good position to benefit from royal appointments. Sir John Treffry was made Sheriff of Cornwall by Henry VII and had accompanied Sir Richard Edgcumbe on his diplomatic mission to Ireland. William Treffry gained the lucrative post of surveyor of customs and controller of coinage of tin in Devon and Cornwall and in 1533 his son Thomas became collector of customs in the ports of Plymouth and Fowey.[22] These types of appointments gave the holder valuable income and power.

At this time Tywardreath Priory was still in existence. After suffering in the late fourteenth century it had managed to survive better under Henry V as its French prior, John Roger, made himself useful to the King. The next prior was an Englishman and he was followed by Walter Barnecut who regained its staffing of seven monks. It had also been supported by the local gentry such as Treffrys, Bevills, Grenvilles and Tregians. By the time of Henry VIII it was well established as a Benedictine priory and had an annual income of £200. The Tywardreath priory's income came mainly from unspecified but lucrative dues in Fowey.[23] Henry had, however, another plan for the priory as part of the dissolution of the monasteries and a letter came from his chief minister, Thomas Cromwell to the Prior.

The King hears that the town of Fowey is sore decayed, partly because there is no order of justice there, as the liberties granted by the King and his progenitors to the Prior and his predecessors, and by them to the inhabitants of the town, remain in his hands... The King thinks that Fowey ought to be his, and holden of him, and intends that it shall be provided with good governance and for defence against foreign enemies; to which the Prior has had little regard, nor yet to the good rule of himself and his monastery. The King thinks that he is very unworthy to have rule of any town, that cannot well rule himself. [24]

The bearer of the message from King Henry's Chancellor was Thomas Treffry. This letter was a warning and the next letter closed the priory 'For his highness thinketh that the said Porte of Fowey ought to be his and title beholden of him so that His Grace intendeth from hensforth to have it well provided for with good governanunce and of defence against the enemies of the realm.'[25] This was the only Cornish priory to be compulsorily closed and the rest of the Cornish religious houses rapidly saw the light and folded also.

The income of the Tywardreath priory duly went to the Crown but one year later Treffry made a request to Cromwell for corporation status for the town, the establishment of market days, a reduction in the taxes on wine and various other requests to provide income for the town. For himself he wanted the manor of Trenant from which income he offered to maintain the defence of the town and port.[26] St Catherine's Castle was indeed built as a major fortification at the mouth of the river. Henry also encouraged privateering by issuing a proclamation in 1544 allowing his subjects unrestricted private warfare at sea,

△ Fowey Haven in the time of Henry VIII (from Lyson's Magna Britanica) (British Library)

with no legal safeguards. This encouraged the extension of their targets from the French to any neutral shipping especially traffic between Spain and Flanders.[27]

The succession of Mary to the throne caused the protestant Treffry to leave the country in 1544 and seek refuge abroad, but he returned with the accession of Queen Elizabeth. This was the era of the great Anglo-Spanish hostility and Elizabeth had few qualms about encouraging her subjects to raid Spanish ships. In 1568 a Spanish treasure ship taking £400,000 (a loan from Genoese bankers to pay Spanish troops in the Netherlands) sought refuge in Fowey from French rovers (privateers). While not at war at the time there was a tense relationship between England and Spain and so the decision was taken to embargo the ships. The treasure was taken out and carefully counted in front of the Spaniards and witnessed by 'honest men of Fowey'. It was kept initially at Place House and then taken to London and the money transferred to the treasury. It was eventually repaid to the Genoese bankers but not until the Spanish troops in the Netherlands had mutinied over their missing pay.[28]

It was during Elizabeth's reign that Fowey became a parliamentary borough sending two MPs to Westminster and in 1573 John Rashleigh bought the lands of Menabilly and property in Fowey and Polruan. The Rashleighs rapidly became another notable landed family along with the Treffry family and trade was an important factor in their rise. During Elizabeth I's time the English extended their explorations and a Rashleigh ship the *Francis* was with Frobisher in Greenland in 1578 and with Drake in the West Indies seven years later. This ship would later become the symbol on the town seal of Fowey.

Trade was not always easy as war caused restrictions and the Secretary of State, Sir Francis Walsingham, controlled licences for trade with certain countries such as France. No pilchards, corn, or other victuals could be exported to St Malo or elsewhere in France 'lest it should be conveyed to Spain, to the succour of Her Majesty's enemies.' This centralisation inevitably caused frustration at a local level and some officials ignored the requirement to apply to London as in the case of a local licence issued by William Creed, Deputy Collector of Customs of Fowey. The licence was for Leonard Dare, a local merchant, to transport 54 tons of pilchards and conger in the *Trudeler* bound for St Malo in October 1585 (autumn being pilchard export season).[29]

In a time of war any and all intelligence relating to the enemy was gathered and ports were often the first place in which travellers were examined for information. In October 1599 William Treffry and Sir Francis Godolphin questioned three Irish mercenaries who had arrived in Fowey and the case shows the confusion of nationalities for whom such men worked. Bryan Rewgh, Edmund Garrett, and Terg Conell had fought in the low Countries (Netherlands) for the English then fought for the Spanish. They eventually were part of a second Armada aiming for Falmouth. While the first and best known Armada swept past the shores of Cornwall in 1588 the Spanish continued to send fleets out to attack England. The Irishmen spoke of a Spanish navy of 50 ships and 22 galleys, intended for Cornwall or Ireland, with 12,000 men, divided into four regiments, most of them old soldiers including Italians, Bretons as well as Spanish. The three men had been imprisoned by the Spanish, but had fled to St Malo, and from there to Fowey. From their evidence, it was clear that the Spanish planned to attack Cornwall or Ireland the next year. This was indeed confirmation of news that had been obtained by a Fowey bark that had been sent out into the Channel to reconnoitre. A watch had to be kept along the shores and ships were at risk from capture by many enemies as was the unlucky fate of the *Nightingale* of Fowey. It was captured by a Dunkirk ship but the master Henry Tour was put ashore in Mount's Bay and he reported no less than fourteen similar Dunkirk ships prowling in the area. These were said to be well manned with 90 men in the ship, 40 of whom were Spaniards, and eight pieces of ordnance.

△ Place and St Fimbarrus church (Truran)

It was further reported to Cecil that eight Spanish men-of-war were in the area. They had taken a ship of Fowey, two barks of Lowe (Looe), and two boats, 'one of which they sank, and have detained the master, but set most of the men on shore'. [30] This intelligence information was inevitably accompanied by a request for further men and arms for defence.

Eventually the Spanish threat receded and during the time of James 1st there is the detailed record of a Fowey merchant ship being built. It is the earliest such record. The Rashleigh family were by now well established in the Fowey area and their town house was what is now known as the Ship Inn. The Rashleigh ship launched in 1606 from Caffa Mill was the 80 ton carvel, *Success*. It took nineteen weeks to build and employed 30 men during that time under the supervision of Mr Bilton, the head shipwright. Depending on their skills and experience, sawyers and labourers were paid between 6d and 1d, shipwrights 20d or 12d plus meat and drink. In 1608 the *Success* was loaded with a cargo of nets, hooks, leads and lines and headed for the rich fishing grounds of Newfoundland. Here crews remained for the season living in temporary huts, catching and drying fish. When the season was finished they returned to sell their cargo of dried cod, often to Mediterranean countries.[31]

'A Fair and Commodious Haven'

N 1602, RICHARD CAREW stood on the hill, where the Q memorial is now and he, like countless others, was captivated by the sight of the harbour laid out beneath him.

In passing along, your eyes shall be called away from guiding your feet, to descry by their farthest kenning the vast ocean sparkled with ships that continually this way trade forth and back to most quarters of the word. Nearer home, they take view of all sized cocks, barges, and fisherboats hovering on the coast. Again, contracting your sight to a narrower scope, it lighteth on the fair and commodious haven, where the tide daily presenteth his double service of flowing and ebbing, to carry and recarry whatsoever the inhabitants shall be pleased to charge him withal, and his creeks (like a young wanton lover) fold about the land, with many embracing arms.[32]

The peaceful scene was to change with the Civil War when Fowey was direct witness to the most significant action of the west as the Royalist army forced the Parliamentarians to retreat into the Fowey peninsular in 1644. The Earl of Essex took a stand with his parliamentary army at Castle Dore, but he literally had his back to the sea. The local populace was, in the main, hostile to the army and provisions were low. Parliament did manage to send in some ships with food and ammunition but when the Royalists captured the Polruan blockhouse it became too dangerous to send further ships into the harbour. There were skirmishes along the Fowey estuary. On one occasion according to a memorial on the Hall

△ Looking down to Town Quay (Truran)

Walk above Bodinnick, King Charles I had a narrow escape when a shot aimed at him killed a fisherman standing nearby. There is no record of the fisherman or his death or how a musket ball managed to be shot such a distance. Eventually after Par was cut off as a means of Parliamentary supply Essex realised that he had to surrender. He managed to leave Fowey in a fishing boat and was taken to a ship lying off the coast and then to Plymouth. His 6,000 troops surrendered to the King.[33]

With the restoration of Charles II to the throne the enemy now were the Dutch. The Dutch had become a great naval and mercantile power and were the new rivals to England's growing colonial empire. In 1667 a fleet of 50 Dutch ships under the command of De Ruyter caused a fleet of ships from Virginia to take refuge in Falmouth and Fowey. One report stated that 25 ships had safely taken refuge in Fowey. The Dutch were unable to enter the harbour due to contrary winds but this did not stop them attempting to attack the town. As one reporter rather unfeelingly wrote '...they made several shots ashore, but did little hurt beyond killing an old woman or two at random.' The report then confirmed that Fowey was well protected, 'The place is fortified with 100 guns and 3,000 men, besides two troops of horse quartered there by order of Lord Arundel'. The Dutch eventually sailed away after attempting to capture unwary small boats for information.[34] One boat they attempted to capture was described as a leisure boat. Charles II while in exile had become a keen yachtsman and this small craft may have been an early pleasure yacht.

Under Charles II the Crown was anxious to get a better control of the valuable revenue from customs duties and the Treasury despatched William Culliford to report on the situation in ports. At the time the Customs were farmed out, that is they were leased to individuals who paid the Crown a fixed annual amount while levying the local custom and keeping any profit for themselves. In 1671 the Crown assumed direct control but changing the system needed some careful management and a reliance on good officers in the ports, particularly those at a distance from London. Culliford arrived in Fowey and observed the expansion of trade in the port and also a very badly managed Customs system. The Collector, Andrew Cory, was 'An ancient man understanding little of Customs house business', the Surveyor neglected to inspect ships papers, no accounts were properly kept and the Boatman was a 'careless idle fellow unfit for further employment', the Preventive Officer, who should have been at Polruan, had moved himself to Fowey without permission and was anyway 'fitt for nothing but to be dismissed'. The merchants were taking their goods direct to their warehouses without checking and tin and other goods were regularly smuggled due to a lack of preventive officers. The Collector was further charged that during the period of the prohibition of the import of goods from France (1678-85), he had seized imported French goods but instead of destroying them as required, he sold them for his own profit.[35] As a result of Culliford's report the Treasury dismissed many of the men and moved others to new posts elsewhere.[36] The legal quay for landing imported goods was defined as 'that open Place or Key, commonly known as The Town key.'[37]

Industrial Cornwall and the Problems of War

*I*N 1702 CAME THE accession of Queen Anne and Fowey was still involved in the Newfoundland trade as a request was sent to the mayors of Bideford, Barnstable, Exeter, Dartmouth, Bristol, Plymouth, Weymouth, Fowey and Poole for the numbers of ships planning to go and what protection they might need in a convoy.[38] Convoys were a necessity as this was a century of almost constant war. War caused problems for all trade, both foreign and coastal, as the risks increased and the trading environment became more difficult. Some foreign ports became out of bounds and the presence of enemy warships and privateers disrupted trading patterns. The presence of foreign fleets in the Channel caused anxiety and sightings of great movements of the enemy fleets were notified to London. For example, Dennis Rouse reported from Fowey in March 1703 on the movement of 120 French ships bound for Dunkirk.[39] It was the privateers, however, that posed the greatest threat to shipping. Privateers could pick off unwary merchant ships and the French were highly successful commerce raiders (this activity was known as the *guerre du course*/war on commerce). The French commerce raiding squadrons included frigates and some line-of battle ships. They were at their most successful between 1693 and 1713. Convoys were the safest way to travel for merchant shipping, but they were not without problems. They were slow and could be delayed for months by a lack of wind, bad weather, the presence of enemy vessels or a shortage of suitable escorts.[40]

The tin convoys were a particular case. Tin, for which Cornwall was still a major source, was a very valuable commodity and was transferred in well-built slow moving ships along the coast to London. The convoys assembled at Gweek, Malpas and Fowey and a navy escort collected them from Falmouth then called at Fowey (or vice versa) the tin having been brought down the river from Lostwithiel by barge. Between 1704 and 1705 four Fowey ships can be identified as part of the convoy with an average crew size of five: *Hannah* Master Cornelius Hunn, 60-ton *John*, Thomas Wenmouth, 45–ton *Phoenix*, John Stapp or Slapp, and the 50-ton *Prosperity*, Sam Sergent. Even with an armed escort losses were high due to the effective French privateers based at St Malo and Dunkirk.[41]

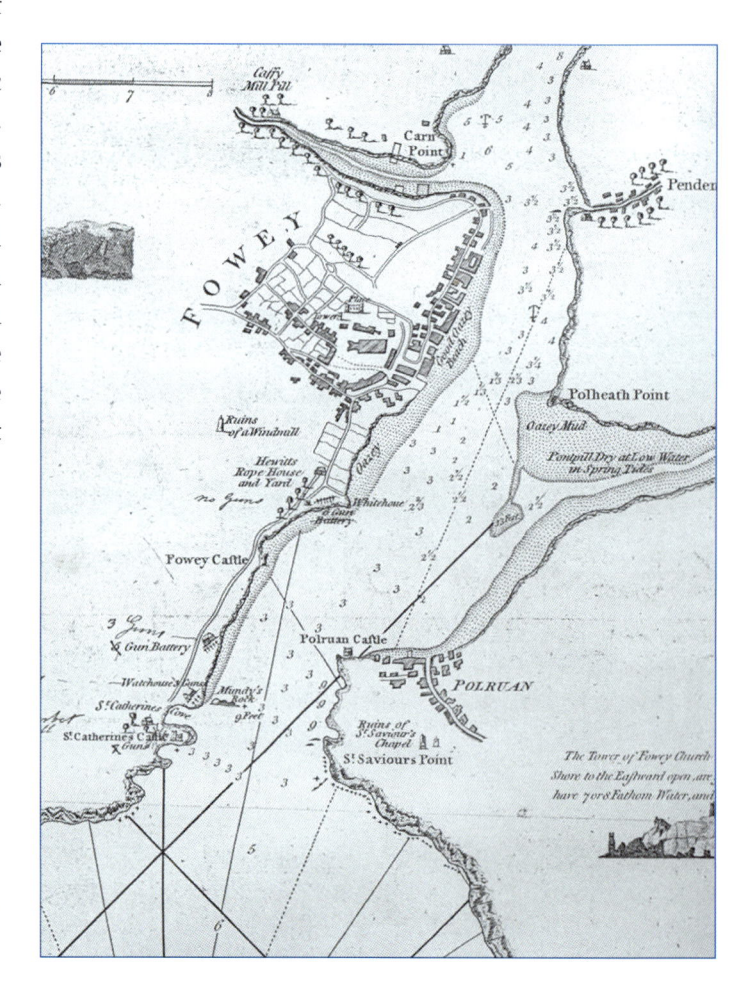

1794 chart of Fowey harbour showing the ropewalk near Whitehouse and the shipyards near Caffa Mill (Hydrographic Office) ▷

The British also had privateers and the Cornish took the opportunity particularly in the American Revolutionary war. One effect of the privateering was that captured ships were brought into Fowey and the ship and contents held until the Admiralty Court agreed it was a legal prize and could be released to the captors for sale. In the French Revolutionary and Napoleonic wars between 1793 and 1815 Cornish ports again sought privateering licenses. Twenty six were granted to Fowey registered vessels, several of which were actually owned by Mevagissey which came under the Port of Fowey for registration purposes. This was the last conflict in which such licenses were issued as it was banned in the Treaty of Paris in 1856 following the Crimean War.[42]

Members of Parliament even prospective ones could bring benefits and Fowey had the right to elect two MPs.[43] The Government had several local positions within its gift and a Government supported candidate or sitting MP, could influence the appointment to some senior positions and would have the direct gift of some of the junior ones. Charles Crokatt a London merchant was such a prospective candidate for Fowey in 1764 and used this advantage when he could. But he over played his hand and in 1765 a complaint was lodged against him by Walter Polgrean who wrote to the Lords Commissioners of the Treasury. Polgrean had been acting as a Customs Landwaiter since 1763 and was waiting for an official warrant to confirm his position, which would enable him to collect his pay arrears. This was given to Crokatt to dispense but he wanted Polgrean to promise his vote before releasing it.[44] Such open use of positions of influence was generally an accepted part of political life at that time.

Shipbuilding had long been an important business in the port since the medieval days of the great wine ships. During the eighteenth century shipbuilding was still a strong Fowey trade as is evidenced by the recruiting of shipwrights from Fowey in 1747 for the naval dockyard in Plymouth.[45] Men were also likely to be more forcibly recruited through the activities of the pressgangs. The men in ports were a natural target, particularly those where the men might have experience as top men in merchant vessels, unlike fishermen who lacked such skills. By the time of the French Revolutionary war in 1795 there was one gang based in West Looe (10 men), Fowey (8 men) and Penzance (7 men) with two based in Falmouth (23 men).[46]

Even with a natural sheltered deep water harbour there was still a need for investment to attract and retain trade as Falmouth was now a serious competitor as a port. This meant improving the facilities for loading and unloading and keeping the harbour free from obstruction. Local investment like this was a particular problem for Fowey as the waters of Fowey were still under the jurisdiction of Lostwithiel, several miles up river. The collection of the port fees was farmed out by the burgesses of Lostwithiel to the highest bidder which led to some curious appointments. Bamfylde Collins, a peruke (wig) maker, held the lease for seven years from 1748 and William Husband, a hatter, took the lease in 1761 for five

△ Ship in Caffa Mill with Bodinnick behind (RCM)

years. It was not a system that encouraged investment in the harbour and with some ships coming in ballast to take out the minerals, the port needed to be alert to the problems of both illegal dumping of ballast and to maintain the depths of the harbour which was susceptible to silting up. But by 1784 it was in the hands of Thomas Nickels a local shipbuilder. His list of ships arriving in the harbour between October 1799 and September 1800 shows a wide variety of ports of origin. There was a Danish brig, a Prussian brig carrying fish and four Norway brigs with timber. English ports trading with Fowey included Ipswich, Yarmouth, Tenby and Liverpool and ships noted as packets or traders from Exeter, Bristol and Jersey. More locally vessels came from Looe, Plymouth, Charlestown, Falmouth and Penzance. Where cargoes were noted they included fish, timber, hemp, hides and bark.[47]

'Ships went to all Nations'

THE NINETEENTH CENTURY OPENED with continued war with France and a real threat of invasion. Along the coast the government formed a group of men called the Sea Fencibles. These were local men, shipwrights, fishermen and others who were formed into groups to patrol the coast. They were paid 1s per day for their duty and, perhaps even more important, they were exempted from being press ganged into the Royal Navy.

With a continental blockade in force, trade was disrupted but prize ships were brought into Fowey by the privateers, smuggling increased and some shipbuilders became ambitious. A survey of shipyards across the British Isles in 1804 showed 29 shipwrights based in Fowey. This is likely to be an understatement as shipwrights, being independent journeymen, came and went depending on the available work. Nicholls was the most prominent shipbuilder in the port at the time, based in Caffa Mill while Geach was based in Polruan. One new aspect of the Napoleonic war was the extensive use of the merchant yards to build warships. The main naval dockyards, such as Plymouth, built only the very biggest ships and concentrated on the essential role of repair and maintenance. Third rate vessels were outsourced to the private sector and the Admiralty preferred to use yards close to their own dockyards. Such was the need, however, for warships that the opportunity to build was spread across the country and Nicholls in Fowey was eager to get his share of such large contracts. He wrote several letters and eventually won a contract to build a 384 ton ship. HMS *Primrose* was launched in 1807, not by Nicholls but by his guarantors as the contract had bankrupted him. The experience may have stopped him from building any more naval vessels but he was soon back in business building merchant ships.

The Battle of Waterloo signalled the end of a long drawn out war and was greeted by great celebrations in the harbour. The end of war tends to be a problem for shipping. While commerce can suddenly flow freely again and former enemies begin to trade once more, ships and men caught up in the war effort are now in the market and oversupply occurs. The town of Fowey might have weathered the depression better if it had not become so caught up in politics. The town could still send two MPs to Westminster but the number of voters was based on a limited number of houses in the town. Whose house they lived in decided how they voted and the two main parties in Fowey were the Greys backed by Rashleigh and the Town Burgesses and the Blues backed by Treffry and his supporters. The Rashleigh and Edgcumbe interests had dominated the selection of MPs and Treffry wanted to break this. The battles over rights were complex and long. Prospective candidates were involved in hotly contested elections and the offers of government jobs, such as Customs places were part of the persuasion methods used. Another rather expensive tactic was to have ship built in a local yard, thus demonstrating the trade and jobs the candidate could bring to the town. One example was when Hugh Duncan Baillie of Bristol a prospective MP had a 281 ton ship the *George* built by Nicholls, a strong Grey supporter.[48]

By 1832 the Reform Act had swept away Fowey's right to elect MPs, a moment celebrated in the naming of a new pub in Polruan named after Lord Russell who had driven the bill through Parliament. Polruan had long been a bystander in the political games in Fowey as

△ Bodinnick ferry and Caffa Mill Pill, 1888 (RCM)

it was part of a different constituency. Now all the various parties turned their efforts to building up the trade of the port. The daymark on the Gribbin was built on Rashleigh land as a navigation aid to shipping, several attempts were made to persuade the government that Fowey should be a bonded port and, long before the building of the Tamar bridge, Treffry proposed a bridge to replace the Bodinnick ferry in 1834.[49] There had also previously been attempts to lure the packet service from Falmouth to Fowey during a strike and charts of the harbour were commissioned to advertise the benefits of the port to 'The Merchants of the United Kingdom'. Copper was exported from local mines and china clay extraction was increasing.

Ships from the Fowey area did not just trade to and from Fowey. A ship can and does follow any trade that brings profit to its owners and the nineteenth century saw an explosion of shipbuilding, ship ownership and trading across the world by men and women in Fowey, Bodinnick and Polruan. One such shipmaster was Captain Tadd who had much to tell his wife on his return from Rio de Janeiro in 1840 where he had taken seventy one men from Liverpool bound for the navy in Brazil. Britain at the time was heavily supporting the navies in South America. Tadd's considerable difficulties in conveying a group of men who had signed up while drunk and then tried to persuade him by any means to return them to England are all contained in a memoir he left with his family. His problems were exacerbated by his own crew who were often in league with his troublesome passengers. He did his best to keep them occupied on the lengthy passage by persuading them to publish a shipboard newspaper, hold concert parties and take part in the traditional 'Crossing the Line' ceremony. Tadd summed up his view with feeling by writing that he would 'rather take an equal number out of the prisons of England than the same lot.' [50] For the master mariner being in command was often a very solitary position so a sympathetic correspondent at home was an added bonus.

The 1840s brought economic depression, which partly explains the men on board Captain Tadd's ship but Fowey itself was also a departure point for emigrants as shown in the following advertisement from the *Royal Cornwall Gazette* on the 12th June 1850:

> ...well-known fast sailing, copper bolted barque ROYAL ADELAIDE would be sailing from Fowey to Quebec about the 3rd of August wind and weather being favourable. The ship was fitted up in the most convenient and comfortable manner for passengers and offered a desirable opportunity to persons about to emigrate. Would be emigrants were invited to apply to the Captain on board, to Mr Bate, Postmaster and Licensed Emigration Agent at Fowey, or to Mr John Hicks, Merchant of Hall. Each passenger would be supplied with provisions as enumerated in the Passengers Act.

The Port of Fowey, like some other Cornish ports, is often referred to as a mineral port and this assumes that more trade goes out, such as clay and copper, than comes in due to the lack of import requirements for a smaller local community. If the port is only measured by its import or export activity this is justified, but it does overlook the wider aspects of nineteenth century shipowning. British trade was increasing across the world and ports such as Fowey took the opportunity to grow with it. The locally-built wooden sailing ship was relatively cheap to build and could sail across the world to any destination following any trade. In Cornwall from 1829 to 1870 the number of locally-registered sailing ships increased at a rapid rate. The number of ships over 50 tons nearly doubled and the tonnage trebled.

◁ Fowey harbour in 1860s before the building of Fowey Hotel (HD)

The main road in
Fowey 1850 (RCM) ▷

This growth was at a faster rate than seen elsewhere in England. Fowey was the port leading this trend and by 1871 it had 140 ships over 50 tons, a total of 14,591 tons, compared to 65 ships, 4,947 tons, in 1829. [51]

Ownership of such vessels was within the local community and the decision to invest required knowledge and contacts and Polruan became a major centre of shipownership. For example the Tadd and the Hocken families were well known mariners and ship owners. In the mid nineteenth century almost every house in Polruan had some close connection with the merchant sailing ships. Around the harbour the benefits were wide. It was not just the shipbuilders and ship investors who gained, so too did the related trades of mariners, innkeepers, victuallers, chandlers, sailmakers, ropemakers, blockmakers, ship brokers and agents. Many fine houses were built on the proceeds of this time of prosperity. Shipowning was a shared risk venture and up to 32 people could own the 64 shares in each ship. In the Fowey, Polruan and Bodinnick area ownership was spread widely among the local residents and frequently there were long lists of shipowners to a particular ship. For a short time in the middle of the nineteenth century Polruan was seen as a place of wealth through its shipowning and the saying was that 'Fowey was the sunny side but Polruan was the money side'. Such expansion attracted men to move to the area with their families and the 1851 census shows the significant number of people who were not born in Polruan, over 50%.

The wrong decisions made by the investors and managers of shipping had serious implications and could lead to the loss of the ship and cargo. The owners of the *Thetis* of Fowey decided not to insure the vessel, a not unusual decision, but a high risk one. By saving on the cost of insurance they hoped to gain from higher dividends. They lost the gamble when the vessel was wrecked at an early stage in her career. The investors, including several women, realised overall 59 per cent of their initial capital investment.[52] Some trades were more lucrative than others. The carrying of bulk commodities such as coal and grain were steady trades but not high margin. On the other hand, specialisation in the fruit trade enabled many shipowners in the area to compete profitably against steamers until the 1880s. *Thetis*, *Jane Slade*, and *Gem* were just a few of the locally-owned ships that brought oranges from St Michael's in the Azores and pineapples and sugar from the West Indies. These ships had to be very fast and they raced across the Atlantic to be the first to bring the fruit to market in Bristol and London in the winter months.

> *22nd December 1873, Ocean Wave (Master J Hocken) arrived in Hull from Livorno Italy with a cargo of marble, pumice, orris root and olive oil.*
> *24 December 1873, Gem (Master W Smith) arrived in Bristol from Palermo, Sicily with 3,850 boxes of oranges*
> *29 November 1882, Dashing Wave (Master Hocken) arrived in Liverpool from the Azores with 2,704 pineapples, 1,033 boxes of oranges and 1 crate of bananas*[53]

Among the shipowners were the women of the port who owned twelve per cent of the available shares in locally registered ships. There were widows like Jane Hayes of Bodinnick, who ran the Ferry Inn. She owned 59 shares in nine different ships between 1850 and 1864. Miss Mary Ann Henwood, a farmer's daughter age 24, owned a share in the *Thetis* and was a regular attender at the shipowner meetings held at the Ship Inn. Zoe Treffry and Emma Davis were other spinsters who held shares in several ships. [54]

Men and women were appointed as managing owners of ships. The managing owner was the business controller of the ship and answerable to the other investors. They appointed the master and worked with him to maximise the earnings for the shareholders by holding

△ Bodinnick, with Butson's boatbuilding yard (RCM)

△ Butson's yard with Harold and Tom Butson (RCM)

down costs and finding cargoes. They handled the increasing bureaucracy and managed the accounts. In Polruan, Mary Hicks Hayes, the widow of a shipbroker owned shares in 36 shares in 16 ships. She was not only buying and selling shares in ships in her own right, but also became the managing owner of the *Perseverance*, the *Gem* and the *Koh I Noor*. She later became managing owner of the *Rippling Wave*. Additionally she held shares in a further sixteen Polruan ships.[55] Like the *Jane Slade* these vessels travelled across the Atlantic and the *Koh I Noor* was eventually lost off the coast of Venezuela.

Sailmakers such as John Carnall of Fowey were regular shareholders in ships as was Edward Thomas, the ropemaker. Another sailmaker was John Edward Hocken of Polruan and his accounts from the end of the century show the range of customers such as Captain Ortmusser with his vessel *Hugo* and several Russian and Norwegian schooners. Over fifty per cent of the vessels in his account book were non local vessels. Many of these were also in connection with the local ship brokers, Toyne Carter and Hannan Samuel plus the shipchandler, Bennett.[56]

Many of Hocken's customers were china clay ships. Despite being some distance from the clay fields, as early at 1852 Fowey was the major exporter to Runcorn and maintained this lead up to 1891 with sixty-five shipments compared to Par's forty-seven and

Charlestown's thirty three. The arrival of the railway to Fowey in 1869 confirmed its position as the principal Cornish clay port. With so many ships arriving came large numbers of visiting mariners and their needs were not overlooked. A Seamen's Rest was proposed in Fowey 1887 and was officially opened in 1890 by Mrs Stopford Sackville who had also donated the piano. The ladies and gentlemen of the committee planned to supply reading rooms, evening amusements and assistance with writing letters for visiting seamen.[57] The need for support for visiting seaman continued and the Missions to Seafarers have only just, in 2009, closed their Fowey station.

Through all of this activity with ships entering and leaving the harbour, one activity never changed from day to day. The Polruan ferry is an essential link between Fowey and Polruan but in 1863 it became part of a dispute that reached the newspapers. Living in Chapel Lane in 1863 was Sarah Pill who was the licensee of the rowing boat, which was the official passenger ferry to Fowey. Here is her letter complaining about unlicensed competition.

Polruan Feb 19th 1863

Sir
According to your request I beg to inform you, further more, respecting the ferry. Thomas Hill has a boat which some person has lent him and is regularly crossing in opposition to me. Captain Peter Tadd has informed me that Thos Hill told him that Capt. Thos Tadd has promised to let him have a boat to call his own and they are disputing Lady Granville right. I should be obliged by your kind interference on my behalf
With sincere and respectful gratitude for your favours
I am, sir
yours most respectfully

Sarah Pill [58]

Polruan from Fowey in 1910 (HD) ▷

The King of Prussia, above the butter market on Town Quay, Fowey, 1890 (RCM) ▷

Such unlicensed activity could not be allowed to continue and William Pease the agent for the owner of the rights to the ferry, Lady Granville, took on the case. It involved lawyers and correspondence for several years before being resolved.

One rather more welcome arrival was Queen Victoria accompanied by Prince Albert who paid a visit in 1846. They arrived in the Royal Yacht and landed at Broadslip which was subsequently renamed Albert Quay in their honour. Other notable visitors by yacht included Prince Henry of Battenburg who frequently visited Fowey in his yacht *Sheila* and Garibaldi, the great Italian patriot, in the Duke of Sutherland's yacht *Undine* and who visited his friend Colonel Peard of Golant in 1864.[59]

Since the medieval ages Fowey had been under the jurisdiction of Lostwithiel who farmed out the management of the harbour dues, essentially letting them to the highest bidder. This was a system that did not encourage the much needed investment in facilities. At last in 1869 after much lobbying an Act was passed that enabled the Fowey Harbour Commission to be set up. The first meeting of the Fowey Harbour Commissioners was on 1st September 1869 in Fowey Town hall. The Rev Dr Treffry was appointed chairman, William Smith represented Polruan and William Warren Dingle and Henry Lambe represented Fowey. The dues were set at 1p per registered ton for every vessel entering the port with cargo. Mr William Hicks was appointed as first Harbour Master under the new system. There was then a negotiation with the Councillors in Lostwithiel who demanded to be paid £45 each year for the loss of their income.

By 1884 the case for loss of dues with Lostwithiel had not been resolved, but circumstances had changed. Lostwithiel was now was seeking support from Fowey for its new charter. Feelings ran high and there was a minority view in Lostwithiel that preferred to give up charter rather than the right to dues. Eventually in January 1885 Fowey Harbour Commission offered a lump sum compensation of £300 and withdrew opposition to the Lostwithiel charter. Lostwithiel counter proposed, but eventually with the assistance of the Board of Trade a decision was agreed at a final payment of £350. On 16th June 1885, over six hundred years of Lostwithiel's control over the waters of Fowey finally came to an end.[60]

In 1874 the Harbour Commissioners were advertising for a steam dredger. Dredging has always been a necessity in the harbour in order to maintain clear channels for larger ships. Steam tugs were also used and the first steam tug in Fowey was the 40-ton *Countess of Jersey* in 1881. An earlier tug *Treffry* had worked out of Par. These were the start of a long line of hard working tugs that improved vessel handling in the harbour as did the continually improved jetties, hidden from view up river from Fowey.

The shipbuilding firms in the harbour never embraced steam, their locations were too small and steam required large amounts of capital and very different skills. The last large square rigged sailing ship, *ES Hocken*, was launched in 1879 and the last merchant sailing ship to be built was the ketch *Rival* from Heller's yard. Many yards closed or remained to build small boats. Just one shipyard in Polruan was left to repair and maintain the last few sailing vessels still active, and to get by as best they could on any work that might be available. By the end of the century many of the old trades connected to the sailing ships were passing. On Brazen Island, once Butson's shipyard, there was now a pilchard canning factory.

△ Fowey harbour from the Esplanade, late 19th century postcard (HD)

◁ A Steam tug towing a sailing ship, the ropewalk moved uphill and the Fowey Hotel is built
(Jim Matthews)

Tourism and yachting increased and local regattas held rowing races and yacht racing began towards the end of the century. The railway from Lostwithiel to Fowey was opened to passengers in 1883, but already the local businesses were catering for the holiday maker with an increasing number of boarding houses and hotels. Second homes were not new either. Whitehouse on the Esplanade in Fowey was built in 1873 for Richard Martyn. Martyn was a major china clay owner and his main house was Carthew House in St Austell (now the China Clay museum).

The Rise of Yachting and Tourism

BY 1902 THE DECLINE of the local specialised craftsmen and the rise of the service industry was obvious in the trade directory. What remained of the shipbuilding tradition were three boat builders and Slade and Sons in Polruan, who described themselves as 'Ship & boat builders, & ship chandlers' supplying blocks, tar, turpentine, and varnishes. The resident sailmaker at Fowey was William Furse, and James Thomas, (the fourth generation ropemaker) was still listed, but a row of houses now stood on his ropewalk. Mrs Thomas was advertising apartments for the tourists. The two largest business categories now were brokers, both ship and insurance, with seven entries, and visitor accommodation, with entries for 31 apartments and five hotels.[61]

Until the end of the First World War sailing ships were still seen in the harbour. Older fast sailing vessel from other ports were bought by local shipowners and traded from the port. Famous names such as *Trevellas, Lydia Cardell, Waterwitch, Helena Anna, Jane Banks*, that had once carried exotic cargoes across the oceans now worked around the coast carrying china clay, coal or timber. Sailing ships continued to work during the war but losses were high and the depression following the war saw many of them taken off the register, broken up or sold elsewhere.

During the war a destroyer and two torpedo boats were stationed in harbour and the last remaining shipyard in Polruan, Slade's yard, was busy with the repair and maintenance of vessels. Just after the war they gained a very large and important commission to rebuild and repair a severely damaged sailing ship, the 623-ton three-masted schooner, *AB Sherman*. It took the yard eighteen months to complete the job but, by 1921, the work was complete and the ship, now with four masts, had passed the highest ship classification survey. She had cost over £6,000 to repair but on her first voyage to Italy water got into the hold damaging the cargo and she was sold for just £500. The ensuing financial difficulties for the ship's owners, Toyne Carter of Fowey, caused the Slade shipyard to go into voluntary liquidation in 1924 and come to an arrangement with their creditors. It was a severe blow not just to the shipyard but also to the many workmen who had hoped for more work.[62]

△ Late Victorian expansion of Fowey (Truran)

△ Fowey railway station with china clay waiting to be loaded, early 1900s (RCM)

In the 1920s and 30s around 1,000 ships per year came into Fowey and the nearby port of Par. Ships came in from Scandinavia, the United States, France and Germany carrying coal and sometimes timber, then cleaned out their holds and reloaded with china clay.[63] Richard Hughes, a Liverpool-based shipowner was a pioneer in steamships for bulk trades such as china clay and he saw the importance of Fowey. The clay shipments from Fowey were so valuable to him that by 1918 he had an office there. [64] The harbour was also used for laying up ships and eight steamers were laid up in 1921.

Fowey employed pilots to assist in bringing the ships in and out of the harbour. In earlier times the pilots had been in competition with one another as the first one to the ship won the job. Later they were licensed by the Harbour Commission and in 1906 the names of the pilots were Moses Dunn, James Salt, John Salt, Mathew Johns and WC Johns. They were all based in Polruan from where they kept a continuously manned look out on the cliffs and it was a requirement that the pilots lived in Polruan for ease of access both of the lookout and to the ships. The pilots signalled to the ship with a lamp. The pilot boat was small, just 20 feet and in this the pilot and his two boatmen might go out five or six miles to meet an incoming ship in all weather.[65] By 1920 there were eight full-time pilots and the pilots needed to be qualified for both sail and steam.

Sail and steam together in the harbour (HD)

The loading books for the jetties show that in 1921 there were 28 different sailing vessels still coming into the port. They brought in coal, cement, sand and ships' stores. Coal was the most important item as it was required for the railways, local industry and domestic heating and of course for the bunkering of steam ships. Both sail and steam ships brought in coal and the total shipments in 1920 were in excess of 15,000 tons. The shipbrokers who handled much of the shipments were Couch, Hannan, Hobbs, Stephens and Toyne. The firms of Toyne Carter and Hannan Samuels were the biggest brokers in Fowey. They were also the local consuls for several Scandinavian countries and the elegant consulate signs hung outside their offices.

Daphne du Maurier's first Cornish home was Ferryside in Bodinnick and the family bought the house in 1926. Smells are an evocative part of memory and forty years later Daphne du Maurier described the smell in the air of 'tar and rope and rusted chain, a smell of tidal water'. The view from Ferryside was straight out across the harbour to the open sea. In the harbour there were small boats everywhere, yachts at anchor and 'more stirring still

◁ Steam ships waiting to load but in the background are the remains of sailing ships now used as coal hulks (HD)

◁ Sail and steam loading china clay at Fowey docks c 1930 (HD)

a big ship was drawing near, with two attendant tugs, to moor a few cables length from the house itself'[66] By the time Daphne du Maurier was researching and writing her first novel, *The Loving Spirit*, in Bodinnick in 1931 there were just two sailing ships still bringing in coal, the 310-ton *Elsa* in January 1929 and the 420-ton *Standard* in August.[67] Some foreign sailing vessels still came in to load with china clay, as did the *Waterwitch*, which was owned nearby in Par.[68] Economic problems were mounting after an initial brief post-war trade boom and Leo Walmsley, Daphne du Maurier's writing contemporary who lived in an old ex army hut in Pont, referred to the severe economic problems of the area when almost every man was out of work or unemployed.[69]

The Second World War again affected Fowey and area as they faced yet another threat of invasion, but unlike Plymouth with its large naval base Fowey was not a key target and indeed was considered a safe area for children evacuated from Plymouth. There was one direct attack on the harbour in 1940 when a bomber came in a daylight raid. One bomb narrowly missed the author Quiller Couch who had a garden below Hall Walk. Another bomb was a direct hit on the boys' school in Polruan. At 5.18, just 15 minutes after the school had emptied and the caretaker had left, the bomb fell and destroyed the school. There were further less damaging raids in 1941. War brought new uses for the harbour and it was used by the Polish navy. Some of the men were billeted in Polruan in the Lugger Inn and the Polish names caused some difficulty. One lieutenant recalls the local solution was to provide him with the nickname Whisky and his colleague was, of course, Lieutenant Soda.[70] In 1943 a larger force of Americans came to Fowey as part of the US Advanced Amphibious Training Force and the place was buzzing with men and naval craft. Gradually the fleet was built up and one morning the local residents awoke to find a strange silence and an empty harbour. D-Day had begun.

The Brazen Island Pilchard Company had ceased business earlier in the century and the site was acquired by the Harbour Commissioners in 1926 and further land nearby bought in 1929. In 1936 eight acres of land were bought by the Harbour Commission from the Boconnoc Estate. Equipment was purchased, men were employed and the repair and maintenance of ships began with the SS *Britten* as the first ship placed on the slipway in 1937. Throughout the war the work of the Harbour Commission and the local shipyards continued with extra pressure and fewer resources. The flow of work varied considerably. Motor gun boats and other vessels were repaired and in 1944 some of the D-Day craft that had sailed for France returned for repair, including five liberty ships. Now the Harbour commissioners needed to think ahead to post war trade for the harbour. At last in 1945 the lights went on again in the harbour and the next task after the celebrations was the difficult and dangerous clearance of warheads and mines, the remarking of navigation aids and dredging the harbour.[71]

One of the businesses that had worked for the Admiralty during the war was Charlie Toms and Sons of Polruan. Charlie was a blacksmith who had worked at Heller's yard in Fowey and then with Rendle, a Polruan smith. Charlie had joined Slade's when they expanded their workforce to work on the *AB Sherman*. Like most of the workmen he was then left without a job when the yard called in the receivers in 1924. Charlie made a deal with Ernest Slade that if he could rent their smithy he could also do some smithy work for them as the yard limped on. Toms worked for the Admiralty throughout the war and then continued successfully through the century.[72] In 1968 they acquired what had been the yard

△ An unidentified but clearly important yacht visiting Fowey (RCM)

Working tugs moored at Mixtow (Truran) ▷

of Slade & Sons next door, it had been run by the Hunkins for many years, and today there are still Toms and Hunkins building in the harbour. An attempt was made to increase shipbuilding and the Brazen Island Shipbuilding Company did turn out one vessel the dredger *Lantic Bay*. The other notable name for boatbuilding was Watty. WH Watty had been apprenticed to George Nickells in Fowey in 1864 and in 1880s established himself as a yacht builder.

Yachting had become a major sporting activity and the turn of the nineteenth century and Fowey harbour was well suited to attract yachtsmen and women. The Fowey Yacht Club has its origins in a gentleman's club established in Dolphin Row in 1880. The first chairman was CE Treffry and the inaugural dinner was held on 8th February 1881. By 1891 it had became the Fowey Yacht Club and subsequently the Royal Fowey Yacht Club in 1907. A new purpose-built clubhouse was opened in 1898 on Whitford Yard, previously a small shipbuilding yard. In 1935 and 1936 the club organised races for the J class yachts. [73] The other club in the harbour is Fowey Gallants which was set up with the express aim of encouraging young people into sailing. In 1972 it merged with the Fowey Sailing club and now works in partnership with the Royal Fowey to arrange races and regattas in the harbour. The rise of the popularity of leisure yachting led to two locally based Fowey classes, the Troys and the Fowey River. The first Troy was designed by Archy Watty and built in 1928 and the first races were in 1930. All Troy class yachts are built to his original design.

Fowey harbour is still today more than just a holiday and yachting destination. From the early years of tin shipments to copper and now clay, Fowey has always had an important role in exporting minerals. Whether by barge or now by train and lorry, minerals came to Fowey to be shipped out to other places. Where in previous centuries wharves were built, they were gradually replaced by jetties and over time mechanisation increased and during the twentieth century the number of jobs for dockers decreased. In the early part of the twentieth century the jetties and the railway line were owned by Great Western Railway, later by British Rail, then by English China Clay and now by Imerys. With the closure of Par, Fowey is now the main china clay port and exports have made Fowey one of the most significant ports in the United Kingdom. While many other small harbours are now confined just to the leisure industry and limited fishing, Fowey has survived as a commercial port. However, the Harbour Commissioners are now operating in a very different world economy to their predecessors in 1869 and one of the new sights in the harbour are the periodic arrivals of cruise ships. Elegant as some of these cruise ships are, for this historian it is the sight of the graceful Troy boats racing in the harbour that defines an important tradition. Against the backdrop of the medieval blockhouses these locally designed, locally built yachts are the direct successors to the centuries of shipping in the harbour.

Acknowledgments

In this short book I have endeavoured to add to the many previous histories of the harbour by adding from my own research and new research by others. I am only too aware of the many people before me who have written about the history of this area. The first book I read, many years ago, was John Keast's *Story of Fowey*. I am indebted to him and the many others such as CH Ward-Jackson, LD Spreadbury, EW Rashleigh, Cdr Henry Shore, Isabel Pickering, Billie Graeme and Jim Matthews and countless others.

△ Modern loading of china clay, showing dust (Truran)

Dr Helen Doe

Helen is the descendant of a Polruan shipbuilding and shipowning family who inspired her interest in maritime history. She has a doctorate in maritime history from the University of Exeter where she is a Teaching Fellow in the Centre for Maritime Historical Studies. She has published extensively on maritime history. She is a Trustee of the SS *Great Britain* and a Fellow of the Royal Historical Society.

Endnotes

1. C Parkes, *Fowey Estuary Historic Audit*, (Cornwall County Council, 2000), p. 9.
2. Nicholas Orme, *Cornwall and the Cross*, (Chichester: Phillimore, 2007), pp.4-8
3. N.A. Ackland & R.M. Druce, *Lanteglos by Fowey: The Story of a Parish*, (Fowey, 1978), p. 11.
4. Maryanne Kowaleski, *The Havener's Accounts of the Earldom and Duchy of Cornwall, 1287-1356*. (Exeter: DCRS, 2001).
5. Orme, *Cornwall and the Cross*, pp. 35 & 69.
6. N.A.M. Rodger, *The Safeguard of the Sea*, (London: Penguin, 2004), pp. 134, 492-497.
7. Kowaleski, *The Havener's Accounts*, p. 72
8. Wendy Childs, 'The Commercial Shipping of South-Western England in later Fifteenth century, *Mariner's Mirror*, 83 (1997).
9. Wendy Childs, 'Overseas Trade and Shipping in Cornwall in the later Middle Ages', in Doe, Payton, Kennerley (eds), *The Maritime History of Cornwall*, (University of Exeter Press, 2011), pp. 2-3.
10. Childs, 'The Commercial Shipping'.
11. Alison Weir, *Katherine Swynford*, (London: Jonathan Cape, 2007), p.96.
12. The Overseas Trade of London: Exchequer Customs Accounts: 1480-1.
13. Ackland & Druce, *Lanteglos by Fowey*, p. 11.
14. Rodger, *The Safeguard of the Sea*, pp. 145-58.
15. Childs, 'Overseas Trade and Shipping', p.1.
16. Kowaleski, *The Havener's Accounts*, p. 8.
17. D.M. Gardiner, *Early Chancery Proceedings*, (Exeter: DCRS, 1976), pp.36-37,55-56, 71.
18. Francis Davey, 'West Country Piracy', *Maritime South West*, Vol. 17, 2004.
19. Ian Friel, 'Devon Shipping' in Duffy et al, 'New Maritime History of Devon, Vol. 1', (London: Conway Press, 1992), pp. 76-7; Gardiner, *Early Chancery Proceedings*, p.67.
20. *Magna Britannia*, Vol.3: Cornwall (1814), pp. 99-112.
21. F.E. Burdett, *The Story of St Saviour's at Polruan*, (Polruan, 1968), pp. 8-11
22. John Keast, *The Story of Fowey*, (Redruth; Dyllansow Truran, 1950), p. 36; Henry VIII: Letters and Papers, Foreign and Domestic, 1533.
23. Orme, *Cornwall and the Cross*, pp. 71-73.
24. Henry VIII: Letters and Papers, Foreign and Domestic, 1535.
25. I.D. Spreadbury, *Brief History of Fowey*, (Old Cornwall Society, 1965), p. 17.
26. Henry VIII: Letters and Papers, Foreign and Domestic, 1537.
27. Rodger, *Safeguard of the Sea*, p. 182.
28. David Treffry, 'Place and the Treffrys', *Journal of Royal Institution of Cornwall* (JRIC), Vol. II, pt.4, (1997).
29. Queen Elizabeth I, State Papers Domestic, 1585
30. Queen Elizabeth I, State Papers Domestic September to October 1599.
31. J. Scantlebury, 'John Rashleigh and the Building of his Carvel, the Success, 1606', *JRIC*, Vol III, pt. 3, 1996.
32. Richard Carew, *Survey of Cornwall 1602*, (Tamar Books, 2000), p. 158-59.
33. Mark Stoyle, 'His Majesties Sea Service in the Western Parts', in Doe et al, *The Maritime History of Cornwall*.
34. Charles II Calendar of State Papers Domestic 1667.
35. W.B. Stephens, 'Corruption and Inefficiency in the Cornish Customs Service', in Doe et al *The Maritime History of Cornwall*.
36. Calendar of Treasury Books: July 1684.
37. Limits of Ports and Legal Quays Trinity Term 29 Charles II (1679).
38. Calendar of State Papers Colonial, January 1710.
39. The National Archives (TNA): PRO SP 34/3/129 1703/4 March 18th
40. Patrick Crowhurst, *The Defence of British Trade, 1689-1815*, (Folkestone: Dawson, 1977), pp.55-56.
41. John Symons, 'Cornish Tin Ships, 1703-10', in Doe et al, *The Maritime History of Cornwall*.
42. David J. Starkey, *British Privateering Enterprise in the 19th Century* (Exeter: EUP, 1990)
43. Helen Doe, 'Political Influence in Fowey before 1832', *Cornish Studies* 12, (2004), pp. 249-67.
44. TNA: PRO T 1/451 1st February 1765.
45. A. J. Marsh 'Plymouth dockyard, 1689-1763', in Duffy et al, *A New Maritime History of Devon*, Vol I, (London: Conway, 1992), pp. 201-208.
46. British Parliamentary Papers (BPP) 1795; *An Account of the Number of Pressgangs employed* and the number of men in each.
47. CRO B/Los 295 Harbour dues of Corporation of Lostwithiel 1799-1800.
48. Doe, 'Political Influence in Fowey', pp. 257-64
49. CRO: R5109 notice of proposal of bridge, 1834.
50. C. Behre Private Collection: Samuel Tadd's letter 1840.
51. BPP, 1871 LXI: *Return of Number of Sailing and Steam vessels registered at each Port of Great Britain and Ireland, 1870*.
52. Basil Greenhill, *The Merchant Schooners*, (London: Conway, 1988).
53. British Newspaper Library: Customs Bills of Entry.
54. Helen Doe, *Enterprising Women in Shipping in the Nineteenth Century*, (Woodbridge: Boydell & Brewer, 2009), p.151, 78-89.
55. Doe, *Enterprising Women*, pp. 144-45.
56. Private Collection courtesy of Mr A Samuels; Hocken Sailmaker's Ledger.
57. *Royal Cornwall Gazette* 22 April 1887; *West Briton*, 18 September 1890.
58. CRO: F/1/294-5 papers, late 19th century.
59. I Pickering, *Some Goings On!* (Fowey; Author, 1995).
60. Fowey Harbour Commission Minutes.
61. *Kelly's Directory* 1902.
62. Helen Doe, *Jane Slade of Polruan* (Truro: Truran, 2002), pp. 94-96.
63. BPP; House of Commons Papers 1930, Pilotage in the United Kingdom.
64. John Armstrong, 'The Coastal Trade in Cornish China Clay', in Doe et al, *The Maritime History of Cornwall*.
65. www.foweypilots.com.
66. Daphne du Maurier, *Myself When Young*, (London:Virago, 2004).
67. H Doe Private Collection: Great Western Railway Vessels Discharged at Fowey 1920-31.
68. C. H. Ward-Jackson, *Ships and Shipbuilders of a Westcountry Seaport: Fowey 1786-1939* (Truro: Twelveheads Press, 1986), p.95.
69. Doe, *Jane Slade of Polruan*, p. 102.
70. Martin Hazell, 'Poles Apart', *Maritime South West*, 2008.
71. Fowey Harbour Commission Minutes.
72. Ward-Jackson *Ships and Shipbuilders*, p 61 and notes.
73. Joan Coombs, *A Fowey Jigsaw*, (Fowey: RFYC, 2000).